Stylish Shirt pattern Coloring Book

Copyright

First edition: First printing

ISBN 978-1517299705

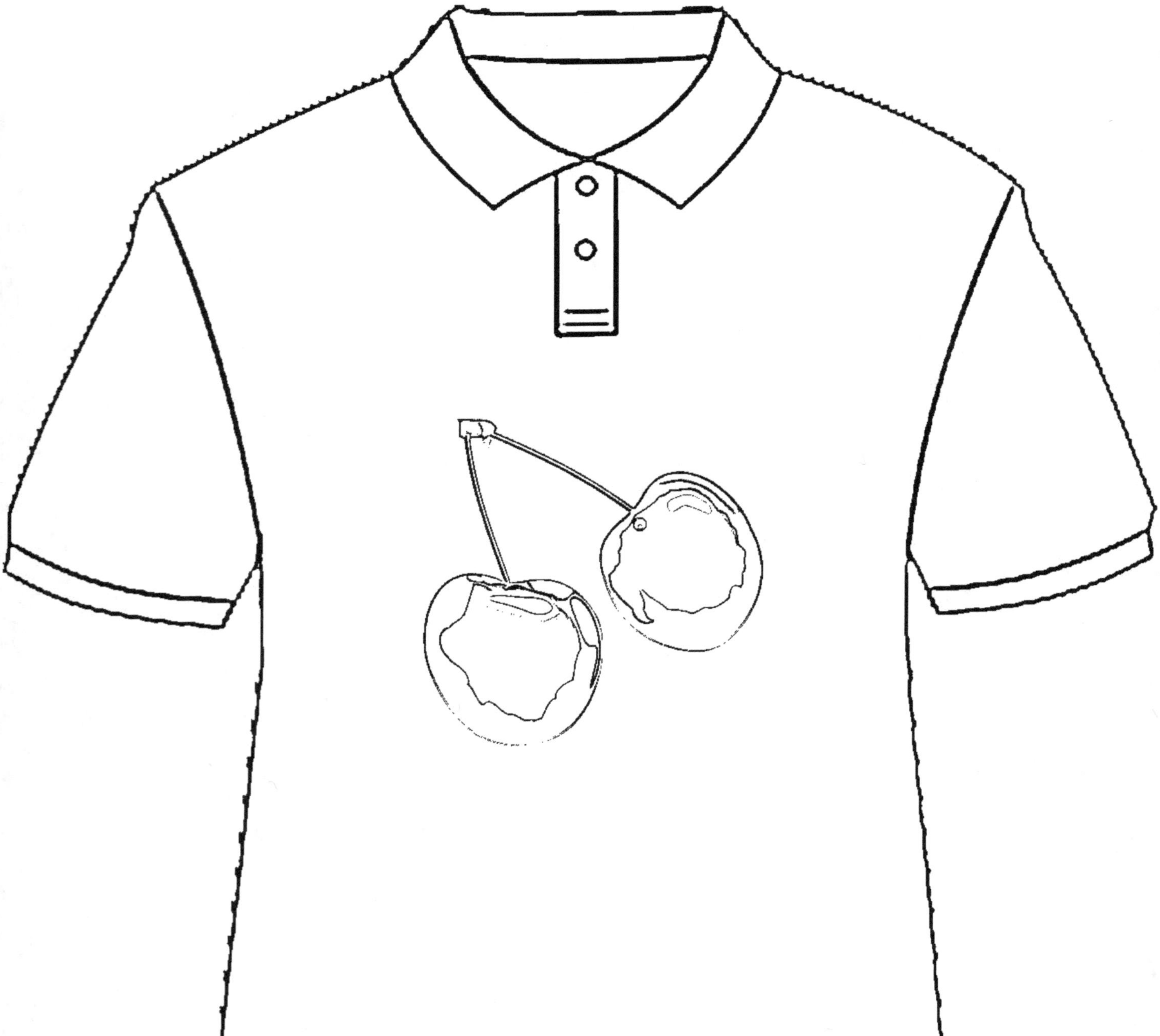

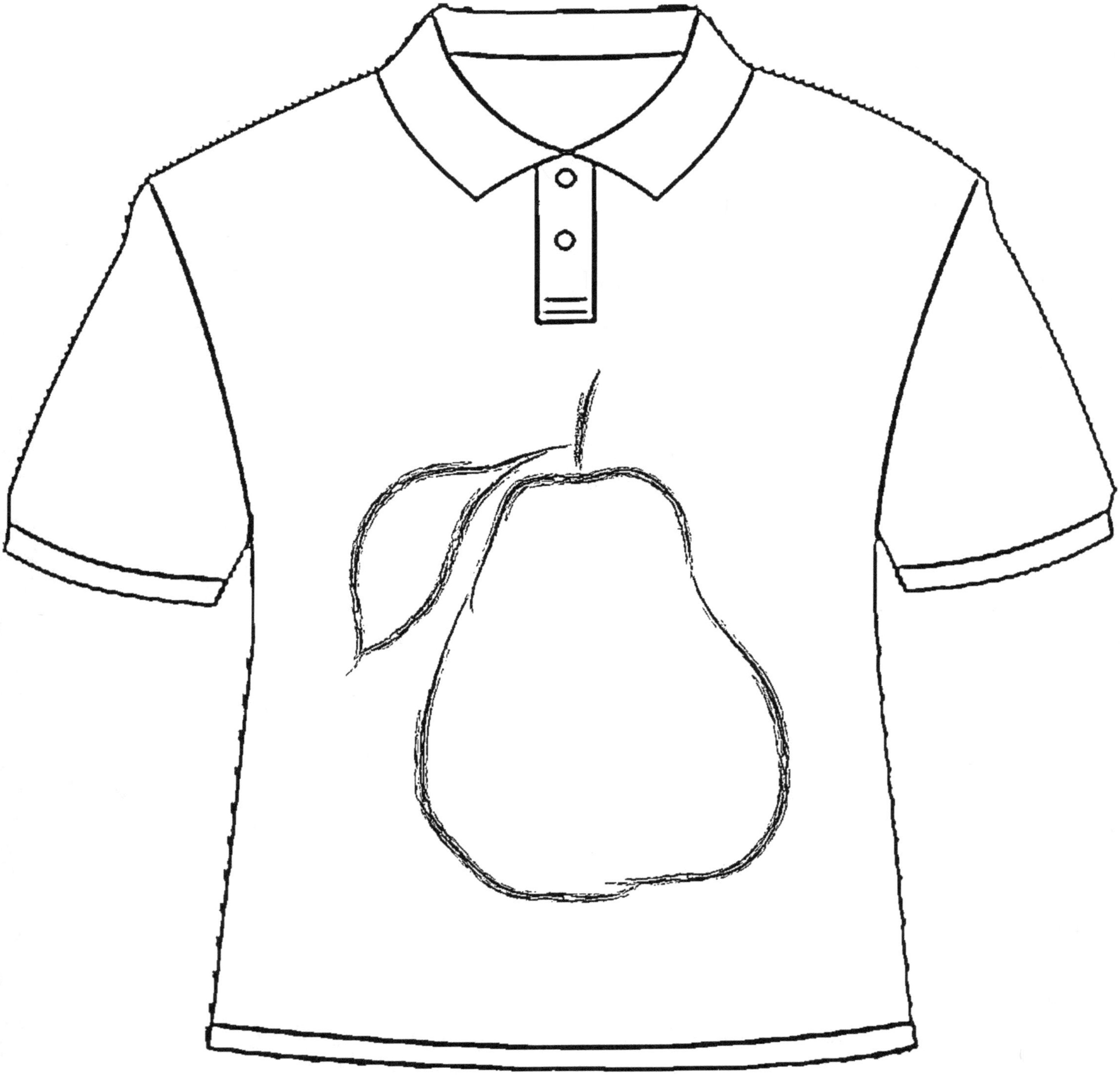

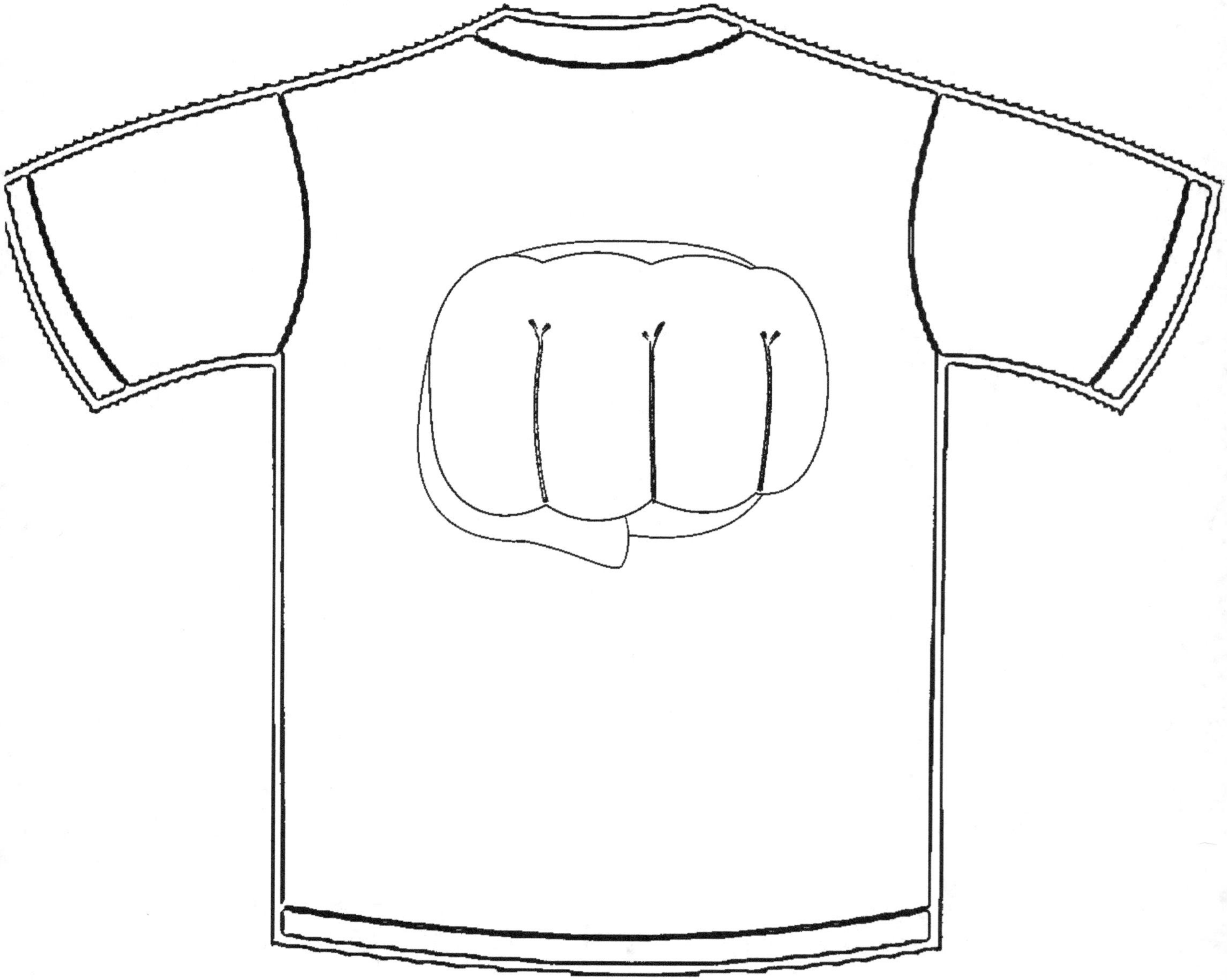

VANGUARD

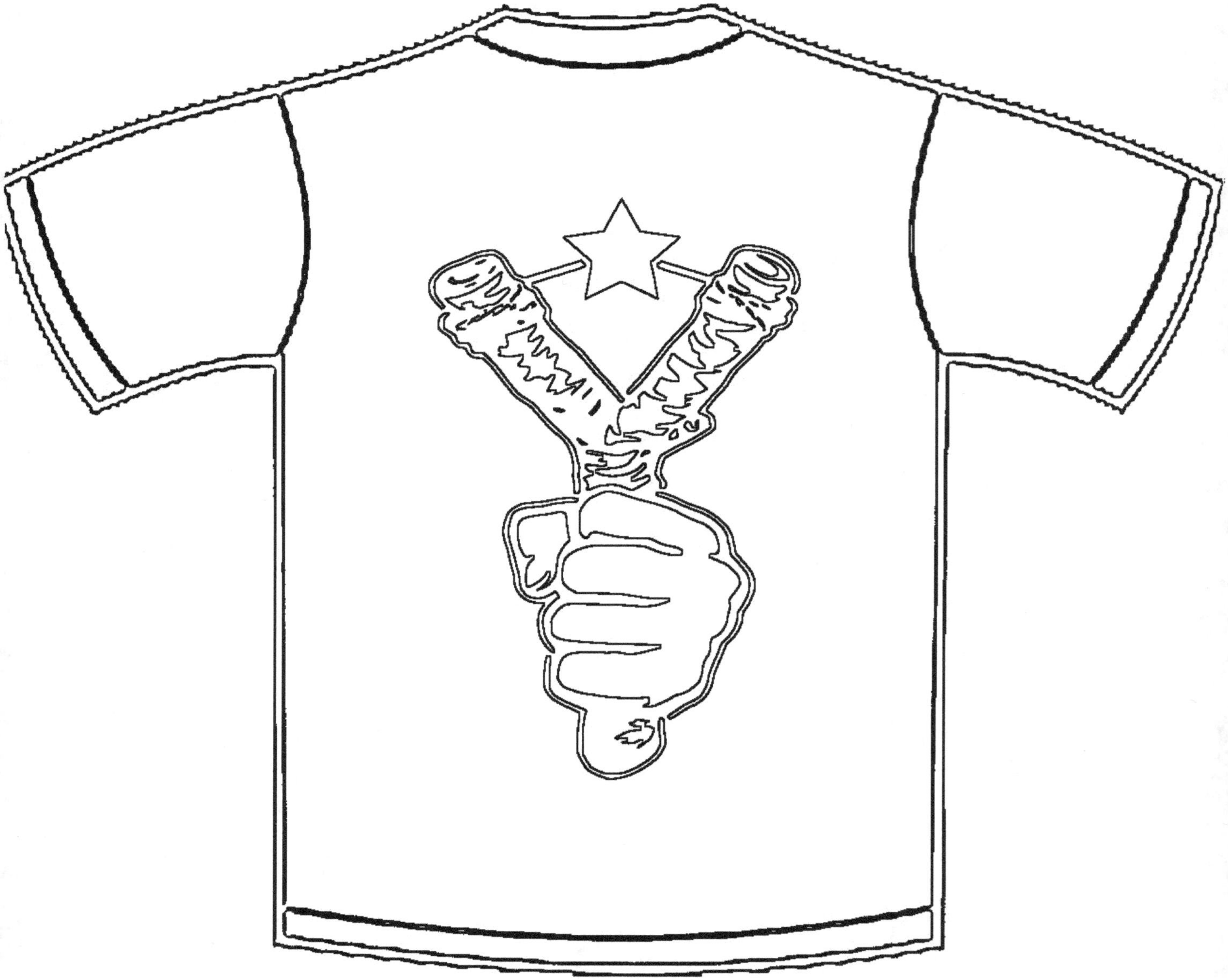

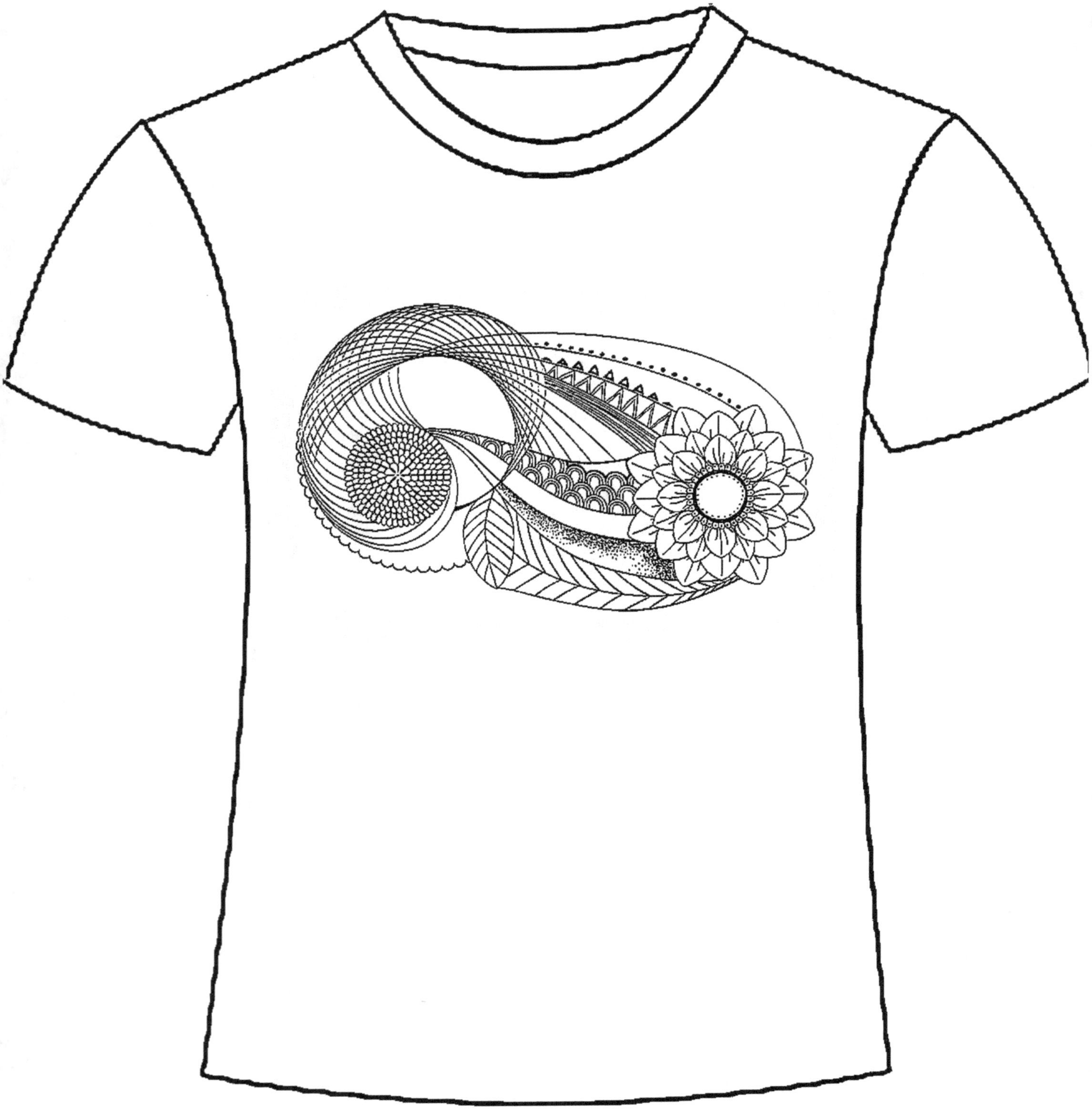

www.ingramcontent.com/pod-product-compliance
Lightning Source LLC
Chambersburg PA
CBHW081153280526
45787CB00008B/3308
* 9 7 8 1 5 1 7 2 9 9 7 0 5 *